I0014461

Blockchains and Smart Contracts for Business Leaders

2nd Edition

Adonis Gaitatzis

BackupBrain Publishing, 2019

ISBN: 978-1-9993817-7-6

backupbrain.co

Blockchains and Smart Contracts for Business Leaders

by Tony Gaitatzis

To Ivy, for letting me get lost
and Lefty, for being a human inspiration

Table of Contents

Preface

Thank you for buying this book. I'm excited to have written it and more excited that you are reading it.

I started working using the Blockchain in 2010 when a friend had me download the Bitcoin app. I didn't think much of it at the time, but I later moved into a crypto-hacker-house in San Francisco in 2014 and soon fell in love with the power and elegance that Blockchain provides.

When Ethereum was released, it became clear to me that we are on the verge of a transformative shift in how business is conducted around the world. It has taken me a lot of time and a lot of conversations to understand the nature of this shift well enough to share it with you.

I hope that this book enlightens and inspires you to explore Blockchains and Smart Contracts in your own organization.

Thank you and enjoy!

Blockchains and Smart Contracts for Business Leaders

Introduction

The Blockchain was born in 2008 when an unknown person calling himself Satoshi Nakamoto published a white paper online describing the concept. Vitalk Buterin added the capability to program contracts into the Blockchain when he launched Ethereum in 2015.

The concept is that there can be a digital asset or currency that is not created or managed by a central authority such as a government. Instead, the users of this currency are the very people that maintain it's value and security, which they do by running a Blockchain software.

Blockchain software creates a distributed accounting ledger that allows all participants to verify both the currency and the spend. A copy of this ledger is stored and verified on every computer that runs this software.

Ethereum made the Blockchain programmable by adding smart contracts, a type of code that can be run and verified by all computers that participate in the Blockchain network. This enables peer-to-peer contracts, asset management, escrow trading, lending, and other agreements to be executed without the aid of a trusted third party.

Blockchain technology has the potential to be as transformative as the Internet. It enables any person, organization, or organizations to create secure digital assets and accounts while securely and transparently tracking the storage and movement of those assets. It has transformative implications in nearly every industry, not only in the financial sector.

This book explains how the Blockchain works and how it can be used to solve today's business problems as well as some potential future ones.

1

Blockchain and the Internet

The Blockchain is an Internet technology. It relies on networked computers to create and validate its distributed ledger. Each computer that runs the same Blockchain software is called a "node" on the network. Blockchain software creates a virtual mesh-network where each node acts as both a client and server, meaning they can both upload and download data to each other.

For asset management to work correctly, all parties involved must:

- Trust each other's identity,

- Trust that the asset is authentic,

- Trust that each transaction executes correctly,

- Trust that contracts will be honored, and

- Trust that no one has hijacked their account.

The very nature of the Internet creates a challenge for these five things that are solved by the Blockchain.

Identity Management

A person can have multiple public and private identities on the Internet. For example, you probably have more than one email address. Maybe one for work and one at home. You probably say and do different things on those two email addresses. Doing so allows you to keep your personal life separate from your work life and it probably only cost you a few minutes of your time to create one of those email addresses. Many people have multiple identities on Facebook, email, and other Internet services.

Having multiple identities enables a person to present a different side of themselves when necessary. Not everything deserves to be in the public sphere, and not all messages are for all audiences. However, easily creating multiple identities comes with a dark side: people can make up whatever information they want online.

Unverifiable information is a bad thing for asset management and contract execution because a person can lie about how many assets they have or how trustworthy they are. They can be penniless or a billionaire based entirely on their intended audience. They can make false claims about their accountability or follow-through. Accounting and agreements are impossible without trusting the claims a person makes about themselves.

Blockchain addresses this by creating wallets. Wallets are an anonymous, distributed address that can receive, store, and spend cryptocurrencies or other crypto coins. These wallets are similar to a bank account. They are a numbered account that holds money or other assets.

Although these addresses are anonymous, Blockchain software verifies the number of coins held in each one. For the Blockchain software, it doesn't matter who manages a wallet, only how many coins it holds. The Blockchain software verifies each wallet and each coin so that people cannot falsify how many coins they have in a particular one.

Verifying the number of assets held in each wallet enables users of Blockchain software to trust that each account holds precisely what the owner claims. Blockchain software won't allow a wallet to spend more assets than it holds.

From this point, this book refers to Blockchain accounts as "wallets."

Asset Authenticity

For many years, people have had trouble with piracy on the Internet. Piracy is easy because digital goods are not scarce; they can be cloned infinitely without needing to procure raw materials, labor, or other costly capital. The entertainment industry is still struggling with this today. Digital media makes distribution almost instantaneous via Netflix, Amazon, and Hulu. It also makes pirated content almost ubiquitous via Torrents, YouTube, and underground streaming sites.

The very thing that makes assets and information so widely available on the Internet makes it vulnerable to infinite cloning. In a world where cloning and distributing assets instantly and infinitely is so simple, there is no way to preserve an asset's value.

Blockchain addresses this by tracking the authenticity of each asset. These assets, known as "coins" or "tokens," are given a unique identifier. Blockchain software verifies the authenticity of these tokens from their creation all the way to the present.

Verifying the authenticity of each token enables users of Blockchain software to trust that no token was cloned or counterfeited. Blockchain software won't let a wallet spend forged tokens or ones that it doesn't hold. These tokens are like any physical asset or currency. They are nearly impossible to counterfeit, their authenticity can be validated, and their location at any time is known.

From this point, this book refers to Blockchain assets as "tokens."

Like money, stocks, or gift certificates, some types of Blockchain tokens are interchangeable with any others in a series. These are called "fungible tokens." Blockchain also has the ability to represent unique assets, such as works of art, identities, or diamonds. These are called "non-fungible tokens."

CryptoKitties is a cute implementation of this concept. Unique cartoon kitties are generated every 15 minutes until November 2018. Each CryptoKitty is owned by a user and no two are alike. Users can buy and sell kitties, or breed them to make new unique kitties. Like real kitties, CryptoKitties are distinguished by physical characteristics such as color, fur length, and shape. People collect these kitties and some are more desirable than others, leading to pedigree-based pricing. One CryptoKitty sold for over $100,000.

Contracts and Escrow

One problem with payments on the Internet is that people don't always get what they pay for. Typically a person must pay for a good or service before receiving it, which creates the opportunity for bad actors to take the money and run.

When purchasing large items in the physical world such as a house, a trusted third party such as a lawyer holds the money in escrow until all parties agree that the terms of a contract or sale have been met.

Smart contracts enable this for payments and asset transfers on the Internet. They can even be used for micro payments or streaming payments - something that was prohibitively costly or complex in the past.

They are written in a programming language called Solidity, and they are infinitely customizable so that any conditions trigger the execution of the contract. The contract can take money into escrow, issue returns or payments, or alert an administrator to disputes. They are capable of working with multiple crypto currencies, tokens, or unique digital assets, and can be integrated into web sites, mobile apps, or other platforms via software-to-software tools.

Smart contracts have been used to create fractional sale and ownership of valuable assets. For example, fractions of ownership of Andy Warhol's piece, "14 Small Electric Chairs," worth 5.6 million dollars, was sold to thousands of buyers in 2018. Each buyer paid a minimum of $4 for their share. As an artist who was fascinated by design as both an public discourse and as a corporate property, Andy probably would have been proud.

Transaction Verification

Anyone who has worked with cheques knows about transaction verification. It takes the bank time to honor a cheque. In the time it takes for the bank to spend the money promised by cheque, it is possible for someone to write cheques for more money than they have available to spend. They may promise more than they can deliver.

Bounced cheques happen because the cheque is not money, it represents a promise to have the bank pay money on someone's behalf. It is a type of contract. The writer of the cheque may not accurately track how much money is in their account and can effectively try to spend the same money more than once.

The Blockchain world calls this a "double-spend." It addresses this by verifying each token spent from each wallet and logging each transaction on a transparent, distributed ledger. The Blockchain software looks at the distributed ledger to verify the authenticity of each token, who currently holds that token, and if the holder already spent that token. The Blockchain software ignores any attempt to spend the same token multiple times from the same wallet. Like an asset or currency, a token can only be held by one account at a time, can only be spent once, and cannot be retrieved once spent.

Blockchain software won't let a wallet spend the same token twice.

Account Security

Because of the anonymous nature of the Internet and the enormous power of computers, it is possible for bad actors to hijack a person's account. For many years, experts have warned about the dangers of obvious passwords and of writing passwords on Post-It notes. Doing so creates the potential for hackers to break into an account by password guessing or social manipulation.

When millions of dollars are on the line, these types of security dangers carry a lot of liability. Large, international corporations have insurance to pay for losses, money to repair distributed relations, and lobbyists to maintain the status quo. Their cost of implementing new technology is more significant than their cost of losing people's money.

Smaller blockchain companies can't recover from such losses, yet are built entirely on new technology. Their technology implementation costs are inherent in their business, and they can't afford to lose their customers' trust. They are incentivized to find better ways to handle Internet security.

That's why Blockchain companies are pioneering and normalizing a lot of innovative security technology. Some of this technology includes two-factor authentication or 2FA, security token technology, automated KYC checking, and advanced cryptography.

By combining these technologies, Blockchain solves many challenges that faced digital asset management when the Internet was created.

2

Blockchain as a Database

At its core, the Blockchain is a type of database.

A database is a collection of data formatted for use with a computer program. It allows for there to be an official source of information that can be updated or accessed instantaneously from any authorized endpoint. For example, employees can update their hours on time tracking website and then HR can produce an invoice from the resulting timesheet data.

Traditional databases store tabular data such as names, phone numbers, and addresses. These databases allow computers to locate information by indexing the rows and columns, similar to how one reads a spreadsheet. This data format is known as "structured data."

Some databases store unstructured data. These databases classify and tag information such as written text, photos, and videos. Up to 80% of Internet data is unstructured, and its classification is a significant problem in data mining and machine learning that is spawning a lot of exciting new solutions.

Both of these database types are centralized, meaning that a single computer houses and provides access to the records. If that computer, its software, or the records are damaged, then the data is permanently destroyed. Any backups are typically out of sync from the live version, so backups will never restore the most recent data.

Additionally, centralized databases rely on a central authority to create and maintain access privileges. Some administrator must decide who can create, modify, or read any part of some data set.

Centralized databases power nearly all Internet services today. Gmail, Facebook, Amazon, iTunes, and YouTube are all powered by centralized databases.

A Blockchain database is distributed. A Blockchain database is one that is continually synchronized and replicated. Each computer that participates in a Blockchain database maintains a redundant and validated version of the database. If any one computer, software, or data is damaged, the data integrity is maintained, and the data remains available for consumption.

Unlike a traditional database, every software that accesses a Blockchain database can read and create data on that Blockchain. A piece of data cannot be altered once it is created. Like a traditional database, additional software can be built to assign different permissions for other software or users that connect to it.

3

Blockchain as a Programming Language

The Ethereum Blockchain supports smart contracts, a type of computer software that is executed by nodes on the Blockchain. This code enables the automated exchange of currency, property, shares, unique assets, or any other item of value in a transparent, conflict-free way.

Smart contracts are written in a language called Solidity and interface with other programming languages via an API. Similar to other languages, rules are coded into a smart contract software that trigger execution when certain conditions are met. Unlike other languages, smart contracts are verified and secure, and have the ability to send and receive money or other assets. Typical conditions include minimum or exact payments, but may include any number of other things such as sending a message, uploading a photo, or voting. Once a node runs the program, the inputs and outputs are recorded in the Blockchain database and are verified by other nodes to ensure reliable execution. Smart contracts have the ability to read and write to the Blockchain, send and receive crypto assets, and hold such assets in escrow.

Smart contracts work a bit like a vending machine. The machine won't work unless a person deposits money into a slot. It holds the money in a temporary vault which acts like an escrow. It is available both for the machine to take as payment for a purchase and as a refund if the sale doesn't complete. If a user has adequate money and selects a product that is in stock, the machine transfers the money to another vault and delivers the product to a receptible for the user to retrieve. Excess money is returned. If there is a problem with the purchase, the machine returns the money from the escrow to the user.

Likewise a smart contract can hold money in an escrow and wait for some condition to be met before delivering a digital product and depositing the money into an account. If the condition is never met, it can return the money to the user. Smart contracts allow people from anywhere in the world who have never met to trade assets of any value instantaneously and without the aid of a bank or a lawyer.

4

What the Blockchain Does

Blockchain addresses these problems by creating a distributed, immutable database, meaning database records can be created and read by any computer running the Blockchain, but cannot alter any record history.

A Blockchain database provides exciting new possibilities for data management. Unlike a traditional database, a Blockchain Database is:

1. Distributed

2. Permissioned,

3. Immutable, and

4. Auditable.

Distributed Database

A traditional database is centralized. One person makes all the decisions about that database, including who can write to it, what data can be read by whom, and even when it runs.

This is fine for organizations that own their own data. But what about organizations that cooperate to manage a dataset or who must be held publicly accountable for some data?

Blockchain databases are a possible answer. A Blockchain database is distributed, meaning that there is no single authority that determines the fate of its data. Each node is contributes to the ongoing maintenance and verification of records by downloading and fact-checking the database. Each node acts as a sort of back-up and security check.

This enables organizations that don't trust each other to trust that data they share won't be shut down. Governments that must share climate data, companies that share inventories, and banks that lend money to each other can all use Blockchain databases to ensure that no one person has complete control of critical data.

A familiar example of how this works is that deleting a sent text message on one's own phone does not delete it on the recipient's phone. Without taking over the recipient's phone, there is no way to delete their copy of the text message.

The Blockchain is similar in that each node has a verified copy of the database. Removing the database locally has no effect on other copies.

Blockchain Permissions

All records in a traditional database can be altered by any account with sufficient permission. Database administrators or other technical persons have permission to add, remove, or alter an entire database, not just one record. The users of the system have permissioned access to records through a software portal to that database.

What the Blockchain Does

For example, Facebook data is managed by engineers at Facebook. The Facebook web software allows authenticated users to add and alter their photos and wall posts, and to view those of other users. This is dangerous because it places the ability to modify records in the hands of people who don't own that data.

It is possible for an engineer or technical malfunction at Facebook to create, modify, or delete the record of any user's comments or photos. This sort of thing sometimes even happens by accident. In 2017 a junior Facebook engineer made big news when he accidentally deleted their production database while trying to implement an update.

The permissions of a Blockchain database is such that only the owner of a record can make changes to it. If a person transfers ownership of a record to another person, the permission to alter the record similarly transfers. Only if they share ownership of a record can they both alter it.

This is useful in cases where a person's or organization's data carries liabilities. That person or organization wants to know that their data cannot be altered without their consent. For example if the fire department makes routine safety checks on a public building that later burns down and are accused of not doing their job effectively, they may want to show a record of their inspections that they are certain cannot be altered by a 3rd party.

Immutable Data

A traditional database is mutable, meaning that records can be purged at any time. The only thing preventing data alteration is a permissioned software interface. For instance Gmail won't let someone change which emails you sent even though they have that ability to do so under the hood. Facebook typically won't let someone change their name due to privacy concerns even though it is technically possible. All this data is alterable by the right authority under the right circumstances. People do this often, for example altering financial records to increase their value during a merger or to avoid criminal prosecution.

This creates problems when critical data is shared between organizations. Data can't be trusted if records can be purged, which makes it difficult for competing companies to share resources in a way that might be mutually beneficial. For example, companies could take each other's in-house accounting at face value during a merger or acquisition, but companies may lie about health of their balance sheet for personal gain making that trust impossible.

Because they can't trust each other's accounting, companies spend a lot on fact-checking each other's claims. Health insurance companies alone spent more than 400 million dollars on accountants and lawyers during mergers in 2016 to do exactly this type of fact-checking.

Blockchain databases are different in that they are immutable. Once created, records cannot be purged, because each node keeps the others accountable. The data can be trusted because each block of data is cryptographically secured on each node. When new records are added to the database, they are cryptographically signed before being copied to each node. Each node on the network verifies the new records and previous ones against the signature before cleaning it. Purging data requires not only breaking and manipulating the encryption on that block of records, but doing so on other computers on the network for each subsequent block while other nodes are continuing to create and validate new blocks of records. It is nearly hack-proof.

This enables organizations that don't trust each other to trust that the data they share isn't purged. Governments that must share climate data, companies that share inventories, and banks that lend money to each other can all use Blockchain databases to ensure that shared data is reliable.

For example, if a group of museums operated a Blockchain database of the pieces in their collections, each could know which pieces the other museums have in-house, on tour, and in what condition. A museum could rent a collection for local display. If another museum discovered a discrepancy in the condition of a piece it could be identified immediately.

Audit Trail

In a traditional database changes happen without a trace. There is no way to know if, when, or how a record was altered.

This is a problem when sharing data because there is no way to know if data has been updated, what changes were made, or when. There is no way to trace the history of changes to know if changes are sane or if records have been manipulated.

In a Blockchain database, changes to a record are permanently logged. This leaves an audit trail of changes that allows for sanity checking of the database. A familiar example is how money is tracked in a bank account. At an given time, the amount of money in a bank account goes up or down, but it is always possible to view the history of changes to that amount. Incorrect charges on the account are easy to identify and resolve.

These properties combine to create a trustworthy form of communication, asset transfer, and data storage between competing parties, without the need for an authority or trusted 3rd party. It enables trusted peer-to-peer accounting.

5

The Origins of the Blockchain

It is useful to know that Blockchain came about as a technology to power the Bitcoin digital currency. The relationship between these two technologies has significant implications for how the Blockchain works.

In 2008, a Satoshi Nakamoto published a white paper in a cryptography newsgroup introducing Bitcoin and how it works. Satoshi Nakamoto is thought to be a pseudonym used by a group of writers rather than the name of a real person.

In 2013, Vitalik Buterin began work on Ethereum, a blockchain that incorporates a programming language onto a Blockchain. This programming language enables software known as "smart contracts" to be run and verified by computers on the Blockchain.

Blockchain is a technology that uses a database and programming language to create secure, scarce assets whose instantiation and transfers can be audited. Therefore, Blockchain is:

- A Technology,

- A Currency,

- An Asset,

- A Resource, and

- A Programming Language.

Blockchain as a Technology

In 2009, the Bitcoin software was released as open-source software designed to allow people to send digital money, or cryptocurrency to each other without the need for a government, bank, or credit agency. The Bitcoin Blockchain stores the record of each transaction and the history of each coin but keeps all the wallet information encrypted. The Blockchain knows at all times how many Bitcoins are in all wallets, and Bitcoins are entirely digital assets, similar to encrypted files.

Each wallet has a public address called a "public key" and a private verification code called a "private key." A cryptographic algorithm produces both and the public key acts as an account number, and the private key acts like a very secure password.

The Blockchain also awards cryptocurrency to nodes that maintain the integrity of the Blockchain, from a limited total supply of its cryptocurrency in a process called "mining."

Releasing Bitcoin as open source allows organizations to implement custom Blockchain technologies to solve problems that Bitcoin was not originally intended to solve. This opens exciting opportunities to adapt Blockchain technology to solve business problems. A business can run one or more private or public Blockchain databases that each perform specialized tasks.

Bitcoin as a Currency

There exists a limited supply of Bitcoin: 21 million in total. Accounts called "wallets" hold some quantity of Bitcoins, anywhere from small fractions to several million. As a result, people have adopted Bitcoin as a way to store and transfer wealth just like a currency. Bitcoin is a type of digital money called a cryptocurrency, and each custom implementation must give a unique name to its built-in cryptocurrency.

Many such custom cryptocurrencies exist and are called "AltCoins" when available for purchase or trade.

A wallet can transfer some quantity of cryptocurrency to any other wallet in a matter of seconds. Cryptocurrencies makes it possible to safely send anywhere from fractions of a penny to billions of dollars anywhere in the world almost instantly, entirely online without a bank or other intermediary.

Because Bitcoin has value, some companies take or process Bitcoin. Overstock, Whole Foods, Dell, Expedia, Microsoft, and other companies accept Bitcoin payments for the goods or services they offer. Some companies process Bitcoin into cash or credit to bridge the Bitcoin economy with the traditional one. BitPay is a company that provides technology that allows retailers to receive cash from customers who pay with Bitcoin. They also offer a special credit card that allows users to pay for items with Bitcoin via a credit card.

Bitcoin as an Asset

Today, traders and collectors treat Bitcoin and other cryptocurrencies like a speculative asset similar to gold or oil. The value of Bitcoin goes up and down relative to local currencies, and exchanges exist that enable traders to buy and sell Bitcoin to each other in a marketplace similar to E-Trade or a Forex. The price of Bitcoin fluctuates as these exchanges allow people to speculate on the future value of Bitcoin and other crypto assets such as KryptoKitties and AltCoins.

Bitcoin as a Resource

Maintaining the integrity of the network requires computer power and therefore electricity, and there is only a small chance of receiving an award for doing so. For this reason, maintaining the network is known as "mining." and miners often share computing resources and the rewards associated with mining by forming a "mining pool" to limit the risk and smooth out the reward of mining.

Over time, the computing power required to mine Bitcoin increases while the amount of mineable Bitcoin goes down. Experts estimate that the last Bitcoin will be mined 2140.

Cryptocurrency is a fantastic new technology that is redefining the banking and trading industries, enables exciting new solutions to other traditional business problems, and creates new challenges for regulation and governance. It has also inspired other technologies that enable automated contracting and escrow, will be discussed later.

Blockchain as a Programming Language

Initially the Blockchain could only be used as a database and a means of transferring assets. With the development of Ethereum, the Blockchain also has the power to run code. Because this code is connected to a Blockchain database, it can hold assets in escrow and transfer assets between wallets in response to programmed conditions.

This functionality enables the Blockchain to act as a third party, trusted to execute contracts and safely hold assets. This functionality is called "smart contracts."

Ethereum also adds the capability to create multiple custom tokens and contracts on the same Blockchain. The properties of these custom tokens are being defined by developers today. These include ERC223 and ERC721. ERC223 describes fungible tokens that acts like money. It can be traded, stored, or spent and each is interchangeable with its type. ERC721 describes non-fungible tokens that act like works of art. None are interchangeable but each can be bought, stored, or sold.

These features combine to make unique asset management and contract execution possible between almost unlimited stakeholders. No one needs to know the others and none needs to work with a bank or trusted third party.

6

Solving Traditional Problems with Blockchain

A Blockchain is a distributed database with permanent record keeping and auditable transactions. Cryptocurrencies are assets that can be transferred securely, safely, and nearly instantly without a central authority.

Blockchain can process a wide array of financial transactions, including stock trading, international remittance, or other asset transactions such as time-sharing or fractional asset purchases. As a result, financial institutions are experimenting with Blockchain technology. However, other industries can benefit from the Blockchain as well.

Case Study: International Remittance

Despite our global digital economy, remittance between countries in their native currencies is a challenge. An example of this is when Filipino virtual assistants perform tasks for American businesses. Clearance times can be several weeks and money transmitters can charge up to 25% to process transactions. People must retrieve their money from a money transmitter store, and in more dangerous places it is common for people to get robbed of their money on the way home from picking up their money.

Blockchain securely automates the transfer of value across the Internet, so a virtual assistant can receive payment for their work in a matter of seconds. More than that, the Blockchain stores that value on the Internet until they cash out. The Blockchain acts like a bank account in this way, allowing the recipient the option to remain cashless in dangerous areas.

Interestingly, the programmability and immediacy of payments on the Blockchain enable streaming payments, so that a worker can get paid for each second of work, rather than needing to work for 2-6 weeks before receiving a paycheck. Streaming payments could allow workers to subcontract to a specialized virtual workforce, allowing them to increase their productivity while reducing their hours.

Case Study: Food Recall

Many farms fertilize their produce with manure, which contains harmful bacteria. They send their produce to resellers and grocery stores in batches, sometimes with small amounts of manure. These companies mix all the batches from many farms and wash the produce but can't guarantee the cleanliness of each item. Sometimes bacteria survive washing, which can make consumers sick. When this happens, food producers must recall an entire line of products. Groceries and resellers have no way of knowing which farm or which batch was contaminated, so everything gets recalled.

If farmers registered each batch of produce on the blockchain, resellers and groceries would be able to identify which farm and which batch was contaminated. They could limit the recall to only affected items, not an entire product line, and could inspect the offending farm to ensure best practices.

According to a study at Ohio State University, food recall costs 55 billion dollars a year in the United States. A blockchain system could dramatically reduce the cost and scale of product recalls and increase the speed with which companies deal with the recalls by pinpointing the source of the problem.

Case Study: Health Records

A doctor typically stores a patient's medical records for one or more visits on a database in their office, or worse, on paper. When the patient visits another doctor, that doctor may not have access to their records, leading to an incomplete history of a patient's health. When a doctor doesn't know a patient's medical history, they are likely to make ill-informed, sometimes costly or tragic decisions regarding a patient's treatment.

Putting patient records on the blockchain alleviates this problem. Hospitals could maintain a private, encrypted blockchain database of patient records. When a patient comes in, a doctor could unlock their medical history instantly for a complete picture of their health and treatments. Doctors would have immediate access to the best possible information with which to decide on treatments.

Malpractice claims cost the medical industry nearly 4 billion dollars a year and contribute to the high cost of both insurance and medicine in the United States. A Blockchain solution would significantly reduce malpractice claims and make health care more affordable for Americans.

These examples are just a few of the many possible ways that Blockchain technology can transform industries. Many startups are working on many more business cases, which is sure to result in a lot of compelling solutions.

7

Solving New Problems with Blockchain

Blockchain is a contract and accounting system that provides a layer of trust previously unavailable between different organizations. It enables instant contract and escrow services, micropayments, and digital rights management on the Internet between anonymous parties.

As a result, many companies are tackling previously unsolvable problems with Blockchain.

Case Study: Shared Spare Airline Parts

Airplane parts degrade with use, and airplanes with broken parts can't fly. Airline companies have low margins, so they can't afford grounded airplanes, so they store spare parts in every airport in case one breaks in one of their airplanes. Knowing which parts will break and where is impossible, so airlines want every part available at every airport, but since parts and storage are expensive, airlines want to keep as few parts as possible on hand to lower costs.

Airline companies address this by creating an alliance that shares spare parts from each of their warehouses. When a part breaks on an airplane, an airline calls the warehouses in that airport to see if the part is available. The warehouse supplies the part regardless of which airline owns it and the bill at a later date.

Unfortunately, airline companies don't manage the inventory and billing very well so remittance can be difficult. The parts have a shelf-life and maintenance cycles which are tracked on paper, easily forged, and often overlooked. Many planes fly with parts that are well past their shelf life or maintenance cycles. These inefficiencies and safety issues waste billions of dollars per year for the airline industry.

Blockchain can solve this problem. A Blockchain database that records each airline part and each repair would enable airlines to instantly look up which parts are available at an airport, how old it is, and what it's maintenance history is. It would be possible to analyze which parts from which manufacturers under which conditions were most likely to fail, and a Blockchain currency transaction would allow the airline to pay instantly or upon verified arrival for the part, regardless of what other company owned it.

Blockchain has the power to handle aircraft part inventory management, safety auditing, and payment clearing all automatically and instantly between companies by providing an invisible layer of trust between them.

Case Study: Conflict-Free Diamonds

Due to their scarcity and value, diamonds are at the center of a great deal of geopolitical conflict. The industry attempts to reduce this conflict by not buying diamonds from conflict zones, which involves the near-impossible task of uniquely identifying and tracking each diamond along the supply chain.

There is a startup that is using the Blockchain to do this. They create a digital fingerprint of each diamond based on dozens of uniquely identifiable qualities, then save that fingerprint on the blockchain. To date, they have cataloged nearly a million diamonds.

They update the Blockchain to reflect the change in ownership each time one of their diamonds changes hands, leaving a secure digital trail of ownership. This makes possible to verify each step in the supply chain for each diamond, and to ensure that each one is squeaky clean.

This same technology can be used to track works of art, expensive watches, and other uniquely identifiable valuables.

Case Study: Distributed Autonomous Organizations

Most investment firms have a small group of venture capitalists who make all the investment decisions. Investors have little or no say in how the venture capitalists run the business, and the venture capitalists make decisions behind closed doors. If one or more of them misread the market or steals from the company, the firm can close, losing all the investors' money.

A new company called the Distributed Autonomous Organization, or DAO is a new type of venture capital firm that is owned and operated entirely by its investors. The Blockchain publicly lists all their investments and benefits from a broader pool of decision makers.

As no one has attempted something like this before, the DAO has experienced growing pains. In exploring this business model, they have experienced and resolved several security breaches.

These are the sorts of risks a company takes when tackling a new business model with new technology.

Businesses can use Blockchain to find innovative solutions to previously intractable business problems. The first companies to try these problems will experience growing pains, but will also build the model upon which everyone else will follow.

8

Potential Obstacles to Blockchain Adoption

The Blockchain is new, and people are still learning how to use it effectively. There will be growing pains, but Blockchain is here to stay. No one is certain what people will do with it or what new features they will implement in the future.

There are several challenges to widespread adoption of the Blockchain in business, including:

- Lack of awareness,

- Lack of consumer trust,

- Lack of leadership,

- Lack of developers, and

- Lack of infrastructure.

Lack of Awareness

The biggest obstacle to its widespread, practical use is lack of awareness and understanding.

A major Blockchain news source, Coindesk reperted in 2018 that 59% of consumers still don't know what Blockchain is.

Before people can develop technologies with Blockchain, they must understand how to use it, and before organizations can implement solutions with Blockchain, they must understand its potential.

Lack of Consumer Trust

Some challenges to innovation and adoption come from consumer trust.

As with any new technology, this maturity and market penetration takes time. For example, Apple released the iPhone in 2007, yet ride-sharing apps became mainstream around 2015. It wasn't until consumers were comfortable with smartphones that they wanted mobile apps for everything.

Lack of Leadership

Some challenges to innovation and adoption come from a lack of understanding of the use cases.

When smartphones first came out, many software companies failed to adapt their services to that platform. Initial attempts to create smartphone apps were nothing more than websites and software modified for a small screen. These modified for the small screen are not the ones that succeed. The apps that succeed are those designed and engineered from scratch for the needs of the smartphone user.

Some Blockchain companies are still in this early stage of understanding, trying to redo their existing business models on the Blockchain. Successful Blockchain products start with people asking,

"What needs to be on the Blockchain, and why," not, "How to we add a Blockchain to our existing product?"

Lack of Developers

Some challenges to development come from a lack of trained developers.

Developers aren't born knowing how to use new technology. Like any technology, Blockchain comes with new terminology, use cases, capabilities, and tools. Just as it takes time to become fluent in a new language, it takes time to become fluent in a new technology.

As such, there are very few developers who know yet how to use it effectively.

Lack of Infrastructure

The technology to make Blockchain easy for the majority of developers, consumers, and businesses to integrate. Over time, developers will learn the technology, businesses will find usefuland legitemate applications for Blockchain, and consumerswill become comfortable Blockchain companies., This will create a virtuous circle that will increase demand for and access to Blockchain infrastructure, best practices, and regulations.

9

Risks to Existing Businesses

Innovation is risky, especially for established businesses. Many businesses rely entirely on market inefficiencies to capture value, so designing new technology to reduce that inefficiency is scary. For this reason, many resist change until the bitter end.

When streaming sites first launched on the Internet, most of the content was user-generated or pirated. Instead of partnering with these providers to allow consumers to pay to watch streaming movies online, they sued consumers, websites, hosting companies, and others. They understood how to sell DVDs, so they struggled to understand that the convenience of streaming movies was disruptive to the DVD industry. When Netflix introduced subscription-based streaming movies and TV in 2007, it spelled the end for companies like Blockbuster who refused to adopt a streaming media strategy.

It's as President Kennedy once said, "Change is the law of life and those who look only to the past or present are certain to miss the future."

Today, Blockchain is forcing banks to face the same type of industry-wide disruption. They capture a lot of their value from financial transactions, so they are disincentivized to reduce the cost of those transactions as doing so lowers their revenue. Banks also have a long-standing technology infrastructure, so integrating new technology is costly and error-prone. They are highly regulated and liable for any losses they incur, so they are extremely risk-averse.

Asking a bank to implement Blockchain-based transactions is the same as asking it to pay to simultaneously change how it does business, take on infrastructure and operational risks, and lower its per unit revenue. This goes against most business's model of raising revenue while lowering costs.

However, continuing without innovating carries even higher risk.

For this reason, many banks are investigating Blockchain technology and tracking its development. Bank of America, Goldman Sachs, and Mastercard are experimenting with Blockchain technology. By exploring Blockchain technology, they can shape its development while unlocking new revenue streams. When one of them discovers an excellent use case for Blockchain, they will already know how to implement it and how to avoid making glaring mistakes. By documenting their discoveries and releasing development tools into the world, they are training future Blockchain developers who are inspired to work for them.

Today's pace of change is rapid. In the last 10 years, smartphones, the sharing economy, and the gig economy have dramatically changed the landscape of businesses in every industry. Blockchain is here. Companies that don't adapt are at risk of disappearing. However, new technology adoption is risky. There are operational, infrastructure, reputational, privacy, and legal liabilities in implementing new technology, especially one that is regulated such as cryptocurrencies.

Implementing Blockchain well requires being open to new possibilities. It requires maintaining open communication with consumers, industry leaders, technology leaders, and regulators about intentions and implementations. It requires the ability to adapt to technological changes, consumer expectations, and regulations all while maintaining a high-level strategy.

What Charles Darwin said about life applies equally to business. "It is not the strongest of the species that survives, nor the most intelligent that survives. It is the one that is most adaptable to change."

In this era of rapid technological change, a business's ability to adapt is a defining quality of its success.

10

Where to Go From Here

Bitcoin emerged less than a decade ago. It's promise of trustworthy peer-to-peer contracts, financial transactions, and immutable shared databases inspire a future where competing organizations trust each other inherently.

Blockchain is a new technology, and its people are struggling to understand its long-term implications. One thing that is known however is that Blockchain has the potential to have a more significant impact on society than the Internet did.

As with any new technology, there are challenges to its adoption and existential risks to businesses who incorporate it into their business without care. Despite these challenges, companies are re-envisioning existing business problems with Blockchain in the hopes of generating enormous wealth.

This book outlined the basics of how Blockchain works, how businesses can use it, and some challenges to its adoption. A lot more information is available on these topics, including those on:

- Research and development,

- Industry news,

- Programming tutorials, and

- Investing.

Research and Development

IBM, Bank of America, and Goldman Sachs publish some of the fantastic work they are doing on the Blockchain, particularly on the Ethereum platform. These publications both help to define the tools and terminology in the industry and to outline use cases that inspire others to push the envelope. Many companies publish press releases or blogs describing their research and accomplishments. Medium (medium.com) is an excellent source for such blogs.

Industry News

Many governments are struggling to define what Blockchain is, how to use it, and how to regulate it. Tracking these decisions is useful as they have long-term implications for Blockchain technology and its development. Coindesk (coindesk.com) and Coin Telegraph (cointelegraph.com) are consistent, reliable sources of such news.

Programming Tutorials

For those who are technically inclined, many tutorials are available online to learn how to program smart contracts and blockchain databases. Ethereumbuilders (ethereumbuildirs.gitbooks.io) and Blockgeeks (blockgeeks.com) are excellent places to start.

Investing

Bitcoin and Ethereum are investable assets. Investing in these assets is a great way to become interested in how changes in the technology and regulations influence adoption and price. One can purchase these assets on exchanges such as Coinbase (coinbase.com) or Gemini (gemini.com) and trade them on markets such as Poloniex (poloniex.com) or Kraken (kraken.com).

All these are excellent ways to learn more about blockchain and its impact on business. Good luck!

Glossary

Blockchain: A digital ledger in which transactions made in bitcoin or another cryptocurrency are recorded chronologically and publicly.

Cryptocurrency: A digital currency in which encryption techniques are used to regulate the generation of units of currency and verify the transfer of funds, operating independently of a central bank.

Ledger: A book or other collection of financial accounts of a particular type.

Bitcoin: A type of digital currency in which encryption techniques are used to regulate the generation of units of currency and verify the transfer of funds, operating independently of a central bank.

AltCoin: Alternative cryptocurrencies launched after the success of Bitcoin. Generally, they project themselves as better substitutes to Bitcoin. The success of Bitcoin as the first peer-to-peer digital currency paved the way for many to follow.

Ethereum: An open-source, public, blockchain-based distributed computing platform and operating system featuring smart contract (scripting) functionality.

Mining: The process by which transactions are verified and added to the public ledger, known as the block chain, and also the means through which new bitcoin are released. Anyone with access to the internet and suitable hardware can participate in mining.

Mining Pool: A way for Bitcoin miners to pool their resources together and share their hashing power while splitting the reward equally according to the amount of shares they contributed to solving a block.

Wallet: A software program where Bitcoins are stored. To be technically accurate, Bitcoins are not stored anywhere; there is a private key (secret number) for every Bitcoin address that is saved in the Bitcoin wallet of the person who owns the balance.

Address: A single-use token. Like e-mail addresses, you can send bitcoins to a person by sending bitcoins to one of their addresses. However, unlike e-mail addresses, people have many different Bitcoin addresses and a unique address should be used for each transaction.

Private Key: A secret number that allows bitcoins to be spent. Every Bitcoin wallet contains one or more private keys, which are saved in the wallet file. The private keys are mathematically related to all Bitcoin addresses generated for the wallet.

Public Key: A public Bitcoin wallet address. Using public-key cryptography, you can "sign" data with your private key and anyone who knows your public key can verify that the signature is valid.

Consensus: When several nodes (usually most nodes on the network) all have the same blocks in their locally-validated best block chain.

Glossary

Smart Contract: A computer protocol intended to digitally facilitate, verify, or enforce the negotiation or performance of a contract. Smart contracts allow the performance of credible transactions without third parties.

About the Author

Tony's infinite curiosity compels him to want to open up and learn about everything he touches, and his excitement compels him to share what he learns with others.

He has two true passions: branding and inventing.

His passion for branding led him to start a company that did branding and marketing in 4 countries for firms such as Apple, Intel, and Sony BMG. He loves weaving the elements of design, writing, product, and strategy into an essential truth that defines a company.

His passion for inventing led him to start a company that uses brain imaging to quantify meditation and to predict seizures, which acquired $1.5m in funding and was incubated in San Francisco where he currently resides.

Those same passions have led him on some adventures as well, including living in a Greek monastery with orthodox monks and to tagging along with a gypsy in Spain to learn how to play flamenco guitar.

About this Book

Blockchain and Smart Contracts, collectively known as Blockchain, are technologies that are radically changing how businesses operate. Although still nascent, Blockchain technology is making rapid strides and gathering a lot of momentum.

This book explains what Blockchain is and what it can do.

Blockchain entrepreneur and engineer, Tony Gaitatzis dives into the business cases and concepts behind Blockchain. This book is non-technical and intended for business leaders, data scientist, and IT managers.

In this book, Tony describes the challenges created by the Internet that Blockchain solves, including digital rights management, identity management, and secure contracts. He explains how Blockchain works like a database and as a programming language, then shows how it can be used to solve several possible and real-world business cases.

Since Smart Contracts transfer and store cryptocurrencies such as Bitcoin and Ethereum, he provides the basis of that also.

Moreover, he gives examples of how Blockchain offers solutions to problems that were previously too costly or complex to solve, opening the door to entirely new revenue streams for Blockchain businesses.

Finally, Tony shares the next steps for forward-looking managers and business leaders to implement Blockchain technology in their organization.

www.ingramcontent.com/pod-product-compliance
Lightning Source LLC
LaVergne TN
LVHW052314060326
832902LV00021B/3883

* 9 7 8 1 9 9 9 3 8 1 7 7 6 *